BONDED BY LOVE

Janette & Ramona's Story

By:K.Moore

For more information, or to book an event, contact :
relatablefictionwriting@gmail.com
http://www.relatablefictionwriting.com

Book design by Nakeia Davis
Cover design by Canva

First Edition: March 2025

Dedication

As the matriarch of the family a grandparent is the heart and soul of the family tree. Their wisdom is the seasoning we need to absorb to grow as a family.

1

Introduction to Janette

Hello everyone I am Janette Marie Jackson-Byrd the only child of Joshua & Angela Jackson. I came from a middle class upbringing with my dad being an electrician and my mom being a nurse. Majority of the time I was on job sites with my dad bonding with my favorite man. Don't get me wrong I loved my mom too but daddy was my hero.

Now fast forward to April 1979 when I met the now infamous Roger Elias Williams. I was 18 and Roger was 21 and after 6 months of knowing him everything went downhill. I really wish I had listened to my parents when they said Roger was a terrible influence. I had to learn the hard way which led to the story that you guys read in the first book.

You'd think that by the fact that he was a year older than me he'd be a good influence on everyone around him. But y'all this story of being with Roger is something out of a horror movie. At 18 I thought I was really grown up enough to make the somewhat smart choice to be with Roger. Boy that experience will make your head spin like it did mine.

There were some good times between us but not a lot as you noticed in the previous books. That guy wasn't even worthy of being called a man. I never got to meet anyone in his family because he said they didn't matter. I figured he just didn't speak to them anymore due to his lifestyle. For the rest of "79" he started drugging me to make me compliant.

Afterwards he would tell me that he loved me and that's why he treated me this way. Now looking back I shouldn't have stayed or tried to make it work with him. Throughout the remainder of this story you'll understand why I act so crazy all the time.

2

The beginning to my downfall

Six months after meeting Roger he changed in the blink of
an eye. One night we were out at a party and he started
beating me when I refused to have intercourse with his
friend Theo. I'm a classy woman and don't get down like that,
I didn't even drink since I was underage. I walked out of that
party and headed back to my home. Roger tried to call me
for the next week threatening to hurt my parents if I didn't
take him back.

Being young and afraid I took him back and it just got worse.
Like I said in the previous chapter the beatings got worse
along with the drug abuse. Then he would pimp me out to
his friends when I was too strung out to put up a fight. By
1980 I didn't even recognize myself in the mirror. The drugs

had taken a devastating effect on my appearance. I could barely hold my body weight up due to me being extremely thin.

I tried so many times to get away from that monster and go back to my parents. I noticed that he had people following me everywhere I went in the city. By 1982 I had hit rock bottom when I nearly died from a heroin overdose. When I woke up 4 days later the first people I saw were my parents. They were so disappointed in me for letting this happen to me.

I promised them I'd do better when I left the hospital, which was my plan. And you know what happened. You got it, Roger found me and the torture began again. By the time 1983 came around I was finally done with Roger. I wanted to tell my parents about their 1st grandbaby. Only to be told by the neighbors that my parents were deceased by that time. They never introduced me to anyone in their families so I officially had nobody to run to for answers.

Even the police were saying there was foul play involved in their deaths. In my heart I still to this day believe Roger had something to do with their deaths just to hold me captive. By the time Zeek was born Roger fooled me for the last time. With promises to Love and protect me & our son I again stayed. My last and final bad decision for me and Zeek was believing those lies.

3

The gift of Love

Once New Years of 1984 came around I knew it was time to get out from under Roger Williams. When we brought Zeek home Roger started the abuse all over again. I loved that handsome little baby of mine and would do anything for him. In my heart I wanted to make it work with Roger but that wasn't in the cards for us. By 1986 I left my baby with a sweet old lady next door so I could get myself together.

Just when I thought I was safe Roger's friend Theo found me and tortured me for the next 6 years. The things those men did to me haunt me in my dreams at night. But I know nothing is worse than the things that monster did to my son while I was gone. When my son found my body in the middle of the street when he was 8 was an act of God.

When I woke up in the hospital, the sight of my baby made me feel like I was finally free.

Just knowing that Zeek still loved me in his heart to care so much for me after being gone for 6 years. When that 8 yr old boy held my hand in that hospital asking me to go to rehab & get better for him something just clicked with me. Next the police came into the room to question me about what happened to me when my baby pleaded with them not to arrest me. I told them everything and that I was going to enter rehab as soon as I got discharged.

Once I was released and went home with my baby and Mrs. Wilson I felt so much peace. I knew that night when I asked her to take care of my son, that I was making a smart decision. It warmed my heart that my son would stop by the rehab facility everyday after school to check on me. He did this for 90 days until I completed the program.

He'd sit and do his homework with me and help make crafts with my roommate. Even when I got out Zeek kept a close eye on me to make sure I didn't relapse. Finding out that Mrs. Wilson taught my baby about the bible showed me why my son was such a sweet boy to everyone he met.

4

Becoming a grandma

Watching my son grow up was a little uncomfortable for me once the girls started showing interest in Zeek. As you may know from the other books,I got excited everytime my baby brought a girl around the house. I was on the fence about Melody from the beginning but maybe I'm overreacting as a parent. Please believe me I wasn't happy at first when Melody announced her pregnancy. But I really wasn't happy when that hefer said she didn't want my handsome grandson Malcolm.

Then there was Destiny who wanted to be with my son but didn't want my beautiful granddaughter Harmony. I don't see why she couldn't own up her responsibility as a woman. We all know that if you lay down with a man and don't use protection "you get pregnant" as your outcome. Or in the case of Crystal(baby mama #3) you get a baby and an STD. I'm very happy that Zeek and Christian tested negative for all

STDs but I do feel bad for the other guy Crystal was messing with.

To most people who read the second book in the first series it would seem as though I wanted to ruin my son's marriage to Kahlani. That is far from the truth. I was just showing my happiness in ways that made the bride uncomfortable. I truly love Kahlani as my daughter and thank her for Camille, Brandon and Ann Marie.

Now Malcolm and Harmony have made me a great-grandma with the introduction of Marquis and Heaven. Those two little cuties are always at my house with Mike and I. Even Lincoln, Kaitlyn, Theresa and Alexander bring me joy every weekend. Max & Cora along with Rashad & Regina made some beautiful babies. I hope they don't grow up to be crazy or just plain stupid from worshiping their own looks.

If only Mike and I had met when I was younger we'd have made some beautiful children. I never asked but I think Zeek would have enjoyed being a big brother. At some point I'll sit down with Zeek and ask him about that.

5

Dating in the new millennium

Like I told you guys already I was a little over the top when it came to my son's love life. But in 2019 when my daughter in-law told me I needed to try dating I was a little scared. I hadn't been on a date in my life, not even with Roger. I just wanted to be rebellious when I met Roger not knowing how controlling that fool was. Yet trying to navigate the dating scene nowadays is weird to me.

Not knowing where to start looking for love I went to the internet like a dummy. I should have just asked my son for dating advice instead of thinking I had all the answers. But that rebellious side of me didn't want to hear my son tell me to go to the church or kingdom hall. So for those who've the other books by K.Moore you know I went to Bumble and Tinder to find love.

That first guy Nate was a lawyer and a complete mommas

boy thru and thru. What middle aged man takes his momma on a first date with him. And what woman has the nerve to eat my food off my plate and think my crazy behind would be okay with that? I had every right to order food for my grandbabies and that expensive Uber on his Black Card. He called me a few more times to go out again and I changed my number every time.

Now let me tell you about Daniel, the doctor who needed to see his own doctor after that date. If this clown read my profile it said "I don't date married men" " No married men allowed on this page". This fool lied to me just to take me on a date. When in reality he was on a date with his wife planning their anniversary and I was the third wheel the whole night. So rather than remind him that I was there, yes I got an uber and left. I could have skipped the doordash but he didn't buy me anything to eat while we were out. I admit I was in my feelings about the whole encounter to go off the deep end maxing out his credit card on a new wardrobe for my next date.

That leads us to Lance the eye doctor that blind bat of a man. Again I ask: how does this man work as an eye doctor but not see his own kids everyday? Then I started to think maybe I should have his baby mama set me up on some dates since she's good at setting him up on dates. But I don't want to be a part of their family drama anymore than I already am for going on a date with him.

Then we have Daniel the retired marine and another momma's boy. We both knew this fool had a food allergy. That's why I asked the waiter to put the shellfish on a separate plate. He didn't need to eat any of the shellfish to impress me. I found it very unimpressive to watch him make himself sick as a first impression. Needless to say I never spoke to him again after that night. At 58 I wasn't going to give any grown physically able-bodied man a bath when he can wash his own behind. And I'm definitely not going to allow his 80 something year old parents to tell me to wash his clothes after he soils his pants.

Now when I was going to give up on the dating game I received a message from Michael that changed everything for me. I'll explain our relationship in more detail in the next chapter for you guys. I know you guys can't understand how that man puts up with me and neither do I.

6

Michael Byrd

My husband was the first man who didn't try to impress me with materialistic stuff. That fine man sat me down and laid all his cards out on the table with all his intentions. I told him my story of being with Roger and going to rehab. When I tell y'all that man was furious that would be an understatement. I've never even seen Zeek get that angry about anything, the veins were popping out of that man's head andI could see the rage in his eyes while I spoke about Roger.

Then he looked me in the eye saying: I will definitely have to see Roger man to man one day. I knew then that it was gonna be a bad day for Roger when they met. When I told my son that there was someone I wanted him to meet during couples night I knew he was the right man for me. He has worked in the same profession as Zeek and would be a great asset to our family. Mike would be the right person forZeek, Max, Malcolm and Rashad to go to for help with their cases.

When the call came about Christian and Camille being kidnapped Mike was the first person to speak up at the table. Y'all know me I was overly emotional along with my daughter in-law. But when Mike took me home and told me to let him do what he was trained to do I was apprehensive. Then when I listened to his conversations and he said those are our grandchildren that were kidnapped I fell head over heels for that man. True to his word that man stayed on the phone getting information to find those babies.

When he told me about the look on Roger's face he told him that he couldn't bother Zeek and I any longer. And when Zeek called Mike Pop in front of Roger in the interrogation room was hilarious to me. Mike said that fool was speechless which made Max and Rashad laugh while he and our son just watched without emotion.

When Roger was executed Mike asked if I wanted him to be there. Before I could answer Zeek leaned over saying: I got it from here Pop go relax yourself. I'm so grateful for this man coming into my life at this point and time. I still have some trust issues when it comes to men but Mike is so patient with me. There were so many times that I thought he would leave after witnessing my antics. But as you can see we've been happily married for 10 years since 2022.

7

My BFF

Now let me tell y'all about my one and only BFF Ramona. We are two of a kind in every way and aspect of life. Sadly finding out that the fathers of our children were BFFs as well was very depressing. Watching our children fall in love was the first thing that brought us together as mothers and friends. Then that trip to Hawaii to meet Ramona's parents made the family dynamic for the Williams family even stronger.

Every now and then I noticed that she was withdrawn anytime a conversation about men came up. When I told her parents my story of living with Roger I could see her cower in fear. I never asked her what Marcus did to her but I can tell it really traumatized her. I prayed long and hard for us both to find true happiness with good men some day. The moment we got the announcement that she had found Jean I was so happy.

All the double dates we went on with these handsome men of ours let the world know we were here to stay. No one can tell us anything because we are two ladies pushing 70 with the bodies of 30 year olds. The only difference in us is that while she's reserved I will slap any and everyone.

Don't get it twisted every member of the Williams family is baptized. But it's still a struggle to put away my old personality when people still want to try my patience. My bestie is good at turning the other cheek but I'm not about to do that so a person can slap both sides of my face. And y'all know I'm talkin about these lonely side chicks who want our husbands.

As you have already seen in other books I get into it with every woman that looks at my husband. Then I torture them with my level of questioning that let them know I'm not the one to play with. I feel like God put us together as friends so I could protect her until she met a good man. To this very day Ramona and I still talk on the phone everyday and I keep her laughing at my antics. I'm sure she'll tell you some of those stories when you hear her story later.

8

Janette's view on Love & Marriage

To close out this portion of the series I want to give you guys some relationship advice. Now when it comes to finding a mate, write out a checklist of things you don't want. Here's my list that I left on the printer when I started dating in 2019.

- No clingy mommas boys
- No baby momma drama
- No open or polygamous relationships
- No benchwarmers (couch potatoes)
- No control freaks
- No criminals

That's just a sample of the characteristics that I can't stand in a man. Unfortunately for me I endured most of those in the first four men I dated after Roger. They were definitely handsome to look at but for College grads they sure were stupid. I never went to College but I have more common sense in my head than those fools.

Then I made a list of things that I wanted in a man that I didn't find until I met Mike.

- Financially stable
- Not in a consensual relationship with his momma
- Not into criminal activity
- A kind-hearted Christian
- Knows how to cook so I don't have too
- Cleans up after themselves

Michael is all of those things and he's easy on the eyes as well. Now I know Chef Jean taught all the men in this family how to cook because none of them could before. Now all the ladies in the family sit back on Sunday nights while the men make dinner. On Saturdays the men clean their houses before sitting down to watch sports together. That makes us ladies very happy since we take care of the house and go to work during the week.

But if all you keep attracting are those from the first list just do what I did. Make sure you're close to his credit card and treat yourself to some nice things. When he tries to take the next girl out and he has no money, change your number before he can call you about it. If they see you in the street just play dumb and walk right by him in the new outfit you bought with his money.

Now fellas in your case you should sit down and make the same lists for yourselves. When you go out to the bar, club, even to church keep on the watch. Look for all the red flags from your "NO" list. You don't have to be rude to the girl but be truthful. If she has a drinking problem and starts a fight with everyone in the building in under 10 minutes, Sir get out of there quick and unnoticed.

Change your number, block her from all your social media sites. Even if you have to move just to avoid the toxic union of being around that person. It may take 4 dates or more but don't give up hope of finding someone. Take it from I was at that point after those bad Tinder and Bumble dates but I didn't give up hope. Mostly because I knew I'd ruin my son's marriage if I stayed single.

None of you guys in the reading world need to be alone. There's someone out there for everyone. We just need to go through a big jigsaw puzzle to find them. Now I'm done being all mushy with you guys, go pick up a bible and letGod lead you to your mate like I did.

Fellas I also want you to know that you need to be a woman's mental, emotional, spiritual and physical strength. As the head of the relationship, you have to be strong in order to attract a strong woman.

Authors Note

If any of you take Janette's advice let me know how it works out for you. Maybe I'll need to start taking relationship advice from her. That's only if it works for my readers

9

Introduction to Ramona

It's a pleasure meeting all of you. My name is Ramona Kapule Ka'uhune-Kekoa. I am the only child of James and Rosemarie Ka'uhune. Being raised on the Big Island of Hawaii was the most fun any kid could ask for. But when it was time for me to go to College I met Marcus and everything changed. Even Though he was an attractive man I was completely blindsided by the person I met on the beach.

From that moment of locking eyes with Marcus I wanted to have a child with him. I wanted a son to be a splitting image of Marcus and that he could be proud of. When we found out I was having a girl we were so excited for different reasons. As you all know Marcus and Roger had sick intentions for my baby girl. I on the other hand was proud to see my mini me as she lay in my arms.

Going back I met Marcus in 1976 when I was 18 about to start College to become a Social Worker. For the first 8 yrs of our relationship Marcus was the sweetest man I ever met.He supported my dream whileI attended College and got my Degree in Social Work. When I told him about my pregnancy we began talking about marriage. Everything changed the moment he looked at Kahlani in the hospital.

When we got home he changed completely and started beating me and wouldn't let me near the baby. The more I begged him to let me tend to the baby the worse the beating became. I hoped and prayed that he'd turn back into the man I fell in love with but that was wishful thinking. When Roger started coming around it was a total nightmare.

I was no longer allowed to go to work so I quit my job to make him happy. That still wasn't good enough for him and his sick twisted world. It was one thing after another from promising to treat me better to putting me in the hospital every time he got high with Roger. The head trauma led to my PTSD and my fear of everyone around me.

10

Life changing decision

By 1990 when my daughter told me what those men did to her it was time for a change. I confronted those two fools about my baby and Roger laughed while Marcus beat me again. From the story that's been told in this series I know I look like a weak human being ,but I love my child and will take every beating to protect her.

That last beating on Kahlani's 4th birthday was the last straw for me. But when I woke up to find out that my baby killed her father was a shock and surprise for me. Then the police and social services wanted to step in and take my child. That wasn't going to work for me so I made a split decision quickly.

After a prayer to the man above while holding my crying 4 yr old. Once in the car I started driving and stopped in front of a building I'd never seen before. The front read **Kingdom**

Hall of Jehovahs Witnesses which peaked my interest. When I entered everyone was so welcoming asking if I needed help. Before I made it to the front Mrs. Johnson was sitting in a chair by the door.

The moment I locked eyes with that woman I knew she was our savior. Asking that lady to raise my baby was the best choice I could have ever made. Letting her know what I was going to do to be better for me and my baby. The smile on that old lady's face was all I needed to motivate me to take care of myself. After explaining to Kahlani why I had to leave her with Mrs.Johnson I was off to find myself.

In the next chapter of my life story I'll let you in on my journey to self love. I'll even talk about how I was able to maintain a relationship with my baby. I'll also talk about my time at Richfield Psychiatric-Rehabilitation center. All the years I've spent there were rough on me but in reality I was being hard on myself the whole time.

11

Mrs. Johnson

Once I was settled into the psychiatric center I wrote to Mrs. Johnson asking her to bring Kahlani to visit me. The first time they walked into my room was on Kahlani's 6th bday. Hearing my baby tell me all about 1st grade made me smile for the first time in a longtime. Then Kahlani started telling me what she was taught at the hall about forgiveness.

I was so grateful to Mrs. Johnson for training my baby in the right way. After being weighed down with the stresses of my past decisions I had one last decision to make to better my life. I asked Mrs. Johnson if she would help me learn the bible. With tears in her eyes Mrs. Johnson said: Kahlani and I would be honored to study with you.

While Kahlani was in school Mrs. Johnson came by to drop off some literature and a bible for me to study. The facility gave me a tablet to use as well but I mostly just read the news on it. On this very day I read the report of my baby killing her school janitor and that burdened me so much. Why do people take pleasure in hurting my baby? I prayed that she wouldn't be taken away for what she had done.

When Mrs. Johnson brought Kahlani in for our study. I felt just as happy as I was the day she was born. From that day on more sisters came to visit me with Kahlani and Mrs.Johnson. At this very moment I'm mostly appreciative of the motherly role Mrs. Johnson played in the lives of me and Kahlani. The fact that she kept her word and allowed me to be a part of my child's life even after she adopted Kahlani.

The day that Mrs. Johnson died was just as hard on me as it was for Kahlani. After years of seeing that woman smile and walk into a room without a care in the world. I almost started to believe there was nothing wrong with that woman. But taking all the lessons she taught me to heart gave me the strength to come out of the facility a stronger woman than I've ever been. I even went back into my career field of social work which I still do in Hawaii.

12

Richfield Psychiatric- Rehabilitation Center

The night I checked myself in was a night I'll never forget in my life. I still had dried blood on my face and all the signs of past reconstructive surgeries shining through my tears. After getting a room and a full night of sleep I went to the group therapy session. I told them my story and there wasn't a dry eye in the room, not even from me.

After talking about my story with the world I went back to my room to lay down. The second my eyes closed the night terrors began and I started contemplating suicide. When the therapist got to my room I couldn't speak out of fear for my life. The therapist told me I was suffering from PTSD but they would work with me.

Within a week of being there they started handing me all these meds butI refused to take them. All the nurses tried to tell me it was in my best interest to take those drugs. I let them know that all I needed was someone to listen to me and a place to feel safe, not meds. Every week the nurses would come to check on me during my study and were so moved by Kahlani and Mrs. Johnson.

One nurse, Jaimie, was moved to tears when we talked about seeing our deceased loved ones again. I let them know that her mother had recently passed away. I asked Jaimieto have a seat next to Kahlani who wrapped her arms around Jaimie in a tight hug. I overheard my baby tell her "don't be sad we'll all see her again". After that day the nurses took their lunch break to come study with us every week.

Needless to say, we made more disciples for our heavenly father. I thought I was overcoming my trauma enough to leave the facility to go to the meetings and I did until my baby was attacked the night of her junior prom. That halted my progress and made my PTSD much worse. We has talked about getting baptized but I couldn't go through with it without my daughter.

I remained in the facility until Kahlani graduated from High School and started College. I just couldn't step foot back into society until my baby was feeling safe. In reality I should have been ensuring her safety but she was ensuring mine while enduring her own trauma.

13

My daughter and son-in-law

Once Kahlani told me that she had gotten her education degree and had found a job I was so proud. I knew it was safe for me to come home from the facility. Within two years of being home with Kahlani she told me that she met a man. After meeting Zeek I knew my baby was in good hands. Not to mention he's a good looking cop also.

When they told me that they were going to get married I asked if he was a christian. Kahlani told me that he knew the bible and they study together with his children. Then I asked how many children he had, only to find out that he had 3. This was my chance to finally be a grandma and no one would take that away from me.

The first time Kahlani brought Zeek to the facility to meet me was a life changing event. The moment that man gave me a hug I knew he was the son I never had. I looked my daughter in the eye during my introduction to Zeek. Kahlani looked so afraid of my reaction to Zeek but I gave her a warm smile to let her know it was alright.

One day in January of 2017 Zeek came to the facility alone in his uniform. I was worried that something had happened to Kahlani and burst into tears. When he sat down and told me she was safe at his home I calmed down. Then he told me that he would love for me to come live closer to them. He even promised to take care of me just as he is caring for his own mother.

He also sat and told me his full life story which made me sad to know he and Kahlani were traumatized by the same man. In the end I was happy to see the man he had become and how much he loved my daughter. Knowing how much my daughter loved children let me know that I only had one thing to tell him. I know my daughter is in good hands with you just as your children are in good hands with her, I said to Zeek with a smile.

Nobody knows this but on 2/14/2017 Zeek came to the facility again alone to ask for Kahlani's hand in marriage. This was so exciting that I had to ask the nurses to help me lookup flights to Hawaii. They didn't know it but I wanted to plan their wedding in Hawaii with my family. So the next year when they wanted to go on a vacation I suggested

Hawaii.

Watching the two of them have two weddings was all the influence I needed to believe in Love again. When I told my parents I wanted to date again they asked me what changed my mind about finding Love again. The answer was simple: "my daughter and Zeek" let me know there is someone out there for me as well.

14

My (New)Grandbabies

The first day of meeting Malcolm, Harmony and Christian was heartwarming for me. Malcolm looked so surprised that Kahlani and I favored one another. Harmony was standing off to the side looking bashful. Christian ran over to me shouting GRANDMA with open arms. To this very day I can't wait to hug that young man. Those children begged me to come live with them saying: "We'll take care of you just like dad takes care of us".

How could I say no to those lovely souls before me in the facility. Even the nurses were moved by those beautiful children. One of the nurses even said that Harmony reminds them of Kahlani when she was young. I can see why that young lady is so encouraging and willing to help anyone. But those brothers of hers are just as strong as their father and well mannered. The way they treat Kahlani and Harmony gave me the strength to feel its safe to leave the facility for good.

By the time I found out about Kahlani's pregnancy with Camille I was overcome with joy. The love those 3 older children showed her brought me to tears everytime we were together. Even during the kidnapping I knew Christian would take care of Camille without a doubt. The boy loved his little sister like she was his own child. Even now when we visit Camille will be up in Christian's personal space if she's not preoccupied.

Camille loves to help me or Janette babysit our great grand babies Marquis and Heaven. Her nurturing role was inherited from Kahlani because the moment Brandon and Ann Marie were born she took over. Zeek and Kahlani have a lot of feel time on their hands because Camille is all hands on deck when it comes to her siblings. All of these babies in this family make my career in Social work so worth every hardship I've endured.

As we continue in this story of bonded Love I'll now talk about other aspects that make me the woman I am today. One of which is (my husband) of a decade. Another is (my career) that I Love so much. And lastly (my bestie Janette) who can light up a room with her comedic behavior.

15

My Husband

Jean Kai Kekoa was a breath of fresh air to come across on the big island. At Zeek and Kahlani's wedding on the beach I decided to stay and reconnect with my elderly parents. At first I thought that was the best thing for me to overcome my past trauma. Within a month my mother told me that I needed to date and she had the right guy in mind. My first thought was that I'm too old for my parents to be finding me a date.

But you know the saying "mother knows best" and that's a true fact in my life. My mother set me up with the man that I have spent the last 10 years with. When I tell you my life has been a fairytale it's not a lie. The first time that I opened the door to go out with Jean my parents were more excited than me. While we were on our date he let me know that my mom had been begging him to take me out for 2 weeks. Talk about awkward hearing that my mom was stalking a man in his 50's to take me on a date.

We got to know each other throughout the evening and that man was truly amazing. Finding out that he was a member of law enforcement on the island for 10 yrs. When I told him that I was going to finish my life goal of becoming a social worker, it made me fall in love with him more hearing him say that he had faith in me and my goal. When he took me home I offered to make him dinner next time. The man surprised me by saying that he was a chef by trade.

Then I suggested that we cook together for our next date and he agreed. Everyday since we've cooked traditional Hawaiian meals together. That is except for our wedding and Thanksgiving weekend. Sometimes we even have a cooking war with my parents on the island. When my grandbabies came to visit last summer Camille created a VLOG channel on Youtube called Family Island Cooking.

Jean and my dad go on there to cook every day while mom and I just sit back and watch. This is my life until we get bored and go to Tennessee to see our grandbabies. I think the next time we go to visit we'll include the other couples in our VLOG. I'm waiting to see how Janette will respond to that idea. As a matter of fact I should call Kahlani and get her opinion. In my heart I'm sure it will be a fun experience since Jean loves being in the kitchen with everyone in the family.

I asked Jean during our honeymoon if he wanted to open his own restaurant some day. That man told me if it would make me happy he'd go open a restaurant. During one of the grandkids' visits Camille told Jean "We need to sell this food to everyone". Jean looked over to me saying "Let's do it".

We let Camille name the restaurant for us and she passed a piece of paper to Jean with a smile. On the paper we read the words "Islanders Tropical Cuisine". As a couple we are doing good for the community around us. Me being a social worker I help the youth to find jobs to keep them off the streets. Jean taught the youth cooking lessons and gave them jobs at the restaurant. We've been recognized around the island for our deeds and asked to expand our business.

16

My Career

Once I was settled in my homeland, I finally picked up the pieces and got a job in my specialized field. My parents were very proud of me for following my dreams. In my time on the island so many children were in need of help. Everyday that I went into the office for a month reading so many cases that broke my heart.

The number 0of young people on the streets raising younger siblings or children of their own. I made it my mission to do for them everything I didn't do for my baby. I called Kahlani to get her opinion on what I planned to do for the kids. My baby along with Cora and Regina came down during Spring Break and the summer to teach these lost children.

Within a year all the endangered youth on the island was preparing to graduate from Middle and High School. The mayor even came by our home to thank me and the girls for our contribution to the youth. I'm so proud of myself for not giving up on myself to make a difference in the life of others. I even put in a call to my bestie Janette since she worked in the rehab clinic at the hospital.

I knew she could give me the answers to how to help those suffering from addiction. Janette made frequent visits to the hospital on the island to have talks with the kids. They all found her the highlight of their recovery. One day during group therapy Janette told the kids to think of their addiction like an annoying heckler in the crowd. One of the kids asked her what they should do to overcome their hecklers? Janette told them to slap their hecklers back into the 1st century "literally and figuratively".

Only Janette can turn a frown upside down in under 2 mins with her opinion. That's my bestie for you but I'll talk more about our bond in the next chapter. But I will tell you that my boss loved to ask me when my family was coming back to the island. After seeing the change in each child I asked the mayor about building housing for them since the shelters were full? Over the years Zeek, Rashad, Max, Malcolm and Christian have helped build 4 more shelters on the island.

17

My Bestie(Janette)

Like I told you guys no one but Janette can make the hard times seem so easy. Even when she nearly made my daughter cancel her wedding to Zeek. When my daughter told me about all of Janette's antics I couldn't help but laugh the whole time. I've never had a friend that found humor in everything, especially trauma. Once we met in person and she told me she really wanted to see our children happy, and she was sorry after finding out what Roger had done to both of our children.

When it was time for our children to have their second wedding my bestie shocked me by firing everyone that my daughter hired to help. But when she returned all the dresses and decorations then gave Kahlani her money back I was floored. That feisty woman is the ying to my yang in life. It's very hard to believe Zeek is her son because they are polar opposites personality wise.

When we both announced we were dating it was a happy moment for me. Yet, every night that she called me to talk about how her dates went I was in tears. I'm sure Jean thought something was wrong with me until I told him her story. I pray for Michael everyday because that girl will drive any sane man to walk away.

When Kahlani said she thought we should have a double wedding I hoped she would disagree. I got really nervous when she agreed but she wasn't as much of a comedy show planning the wedding. Until it came down to the food which Janette forced my poor husband to make just to make her happy. Michael and I kept telling Jean he didn't have to cater all the food but he didn't mind it's what he loved to do (cook) for others.

We still to this day get together and laugh about her honeymoon. I truly can't imagine how I'd react to the things she claimed happened at that resort in Cabo. As you may have noticed Janette and I talk everyday about everything going on in our lives. Even though I may not be able to travel to and from Tennessee a lot, that friend of mine with face-time or video chat with me with all the tea there is to spill. One time she tried to give me tips on how to keep my relationship spicy with Jean.

Now I don't need any advice on spicing up my marriage but I listen and laugh. Janette even calls to tell me about the advice she gives to our grandkids. This is after the kids have already called me with the stories. If you guys have a friend like this, appreciate their company at all times. Lord knowI appreciate all the time I've spent around Janette.

Now I'll let you in on some stories that have bonded me and Janette as sistas, mothers, grandparents and friends. Ladies, you know when you have a friend working in the wrong career field but you don't want to offend them by stating your opinion. Well that's me and Janette all day everyday. I still think that Janette should've been a therapist instead of a desk clerk in a hospital.

To some her advice may be completely hilarious but if you think about it she is right most of the time. We went to a restaurant in LA for our 4th wedding anniversary and of course Janette had to act up. Of course our husbands got lots of attention from the ladies and Janette didn't like that. She told me before we left the airport that she was going to slap someone before we got back home. Buckle your seatbelts for this story.

Once we landed and went to a restaurant on the Boulevard and the hostess was a little too friendly with our husbands.

Mike asked the hostess to show some respect for his wife as did Jean. The next person to be rude to us was the waitress who ignored us as we gave our orders. Now it was Janette's turn to put someone in check. She stood to her feet and told the waitress " you have one more time to disrespect me and you won't be having a good day". Then the waitress laughed and Janette back-handed the girl across the room.

Then when we checked into the hotel Janette got into it with the clerk and the maid. We all watched as Janette let that young lady know who she and I were to the men she was flirting with. When that girl rolled her eyes at Janette even I got whiplash from how fast Janette slapped that girl. Then the manager came to see what the issue was and I told him how rude and disrespectful she was to us. After he finished our check-in he turned to the girl and told her she was suspended for a week.

Apparently she contacted the cleaning staff telling them to mess with us again. By the time we got to our rooms there was a maid in each room going through our belongings. The maid in my room was concealing my new lingerie on her cart. The maid in Janette's room was again stealing Mike's underwear and putting lipstick on his shirts. Since we had an adjoining room both of the maids jumped in fear when Janette yelled " why do you heifers keep testing my patience"? Then she proceeded to hand down that whoopin before stepping into my room to whoop that maid also.

Janette beat those girls like they were her kids with all F's on their report card. Then came Mike's favorite thing about Janette(her interrogation techniques) which I found to be just as hilarious. You'd think since we're both married to retired cops they'd do all the questioning, but no that's not the case. My bestie tied them up with two pairs of my pantyhose and started her line of questioning.

> 1)Who told you to come clean these two rooms while we were checking in? The rooms should've been clean before we got off the plane. 2) Is going through other people's belongings part of your job description? Because downstairs according to your manager it is not, it can cost you your employment. 3) Did you think being rude to me and my best friend was going to get you a bigger tip or sexual favors with our husbands? As you just learned, thinking like that will get you hurt messing with me. 4) Did you get your job by lying on your back? If you did then Mona you better let her keep those clothes she took, them things are probably contaminated with every STD known to man.

Next Janette walked over to the girls telling them to stop all the crying, it's making her head hurt. Followed by her asking them to answer each of her questions now and not lie to her. Because if they did they would receive another beating at her hand. Both of the ladies looked at one another to come up with the answers. Janette got impatient and picked up a bible and hit both girls upside the head.

Janette told them to start talking now or she'd keep hitting them with the bible. The maid that was in my room admitted that the terminated clerk put them up to it. The second maid said that the clerk told them to take anything that looked expensive so we could sell it later for extra money. Upon hearing this news Janette untied them and started chasing them down the hall while hitting with the bible and a belt simultaneously.

All the other guests came into the hall to see what was going on. I called Zeek and Kahlani to spill the tea and have a good laugh. For the rest of our trip Janette told everyone how she hit those two maids with bible knowledge of what happens when you mess with her.

18

My extended family

My daughter and son-in-law have some great friends around them. From the friends in the congregation to their friends at work. Rashad and Max along with their wives refer to Janette & I as mom. Not to mention Malcolm and Harmony's spouses refer to us as grandma. Let me not forget our great-grand babies Marquis and Heaven. I can't forget Desiree Christians future wife. She reminds me so much of my daughter.

Whenever Jean and I are in town I sit with Desiree and Kapri to let them know they can call me anytime if they want to talk. This grandma is always available to talk. But if they want a good laugh they can always call Janette. Those two seem to be suffering from some self-esteem issues. I talked to Kapri's mom when she came to help them with Marquis for three months. I hope to catch up with Desiree's mom one day when Jean and I are back in TN.

At some point all the ladies need to have a girls day to do some team building exercises. I'll even tell Jean to get the guys together to do the same thing. Maybe we'll make it a Bachelor & Bachelorette party for Christian and Desiree since they're next in the family to wed. But my favorite thing to do is watch my family grow and I can't wait until to see Christian and Desiree's wedding and see them build their own family.

Seeing Max and Cora with the triplets is so cute even though Max calls my son-in-law for parenting advice every week. Rashad is even funnier with his questions and Zeek is so patient with his friends. I guess Cora and Regina are meant to be moms since they're school teachers. I love watching them manage those kids and their careers.

Hearing Lincoln, Theresa, Kaitlyn and Alex call me G-ma is so special. I hold those moments near and dear to my heart. I know my daughter says this but I'm going to say it now " I feel so complete with friends that are just as close as family to me". Guys I'm tired from crying and telling this story of my life. So ;ets closeout this book with some more words from Janette. I know she's itching to make us laugh again and she will not disappoint.

How could I forget about Dametrius and Jazzlene. Those two are just the cutest couple. They remind me so much of Zeek and Kahlani when they come around. I encouraged Dametrius to go have family therapy to rebuild his relationship with his mom. We felt so bad for that young man finding out the truth of how he was brought up and finding out he was being used as a pawn against my daughter and granddaughter.

I haven't spoken to Dametrius and Jazz in a while so I hope all is well with them. But I'll ask Harmony and Travion if they've heard from the two. Now that I've finally talked about my bond with everyone in the cast of characters in this book collection, I'm officially leaving now to be with my husband.   Maybe we'll do some couples cooking dates. We might even go hang out with Mike and Janette for a while.

We're going to let the men talk to you guys for a while so we can relax. We're going to go ahead and hear about the bond between PopPop / TuTu Kane with the family. They may not have a lot to say since most of the time they just laugh at Janette. Mike most of the time is at the station with the boys. Jean is mostly in the kitchen with the kids or our staff at the restaurant.

19

A Grandpa's Love

I'm Michael Joseph Byrd former Police Chief of Richfield, TN. I've never had any children with any of the women I've met in my life. I took a chance on a dating app in 2019 where I met my wife. On our first date she introduced me to my now son Zeek. Finding out that he works out of the same station I used to run.

Having a daughter-in-law with a heart of gold made me proud. The night of the kidnapping made me feel that those grandbabies were as much mine as they were Janette's. I had to find them even if Zeek didn't want my help. I see Rashad and Max as my sons as well, we have such a good time when we get around each other. We have a bond in and outside of the police force.

When I said we should have put Janette on the force I meant every word. My baby is the most entertaining when it comes to questioning a suspect. If you have someone around you that's like my wife keep them close because there's never a dull moment with them.

Even my great-grand babies Heaven and Marquis are a joy to have around. But I think Camille believes they are hers only. It's so beautiful to see how thaat princess loves on every little person that crosses her path. I honestly think Camille is going to follow in the footsteps of her mother and big sister in the education field. On another note my brother in arms Jean is a great person to call a friend.

That man taught me and all the guys how to cook for our wives. Everytime the girls complain about needing a break we get together to make all their meals. In book 10 each of the fellas will tell you what we do for our women. Maybe we'll give you readers some relationship advice to keep your lady happy. Now my friend Jean would like to speak to you guys before we transsion into book 9.

I Jean Kai Kekoa is the husband of Ramona and the dad of Kahlani. That young lady is a blessing and I'm proud to be apart of her family. Giving the fact that I never had childrenbefore meeting Ramona, Kahlani makes me feel like I've been her father my whole life. Watching her be a mother has given me such pride in my choice to marry her mother.

All 6 of my grandbabies are a joy to watch grow up. Whenever Zeek and Kahlani needed some time to themselves it was a privilege to watch over those children. Even if we were just in town for a short visit I couldn't wait to see those babies. I have to agree with Mike about our great-grand babies Marquis and Heaven. Those two munchkins are a complete delight to be around.

That is if Camille will let you be around them. I think she believes she's their parent and we're just bestanders when we come to visit. I don't what Camille will be like in her teens but I hope she doesn't change. Brandon and Ann Marie are the most independent children I've ever met just brilliant rays of light.

Next I can't forget about the extended family Kapri, Travion, Desiree, Dametrius and Jazzlene. All of them are such good christians and friends to the members of this family. Those young people have been great friends to Malcolm and Harmany. Seeing them all have successful marriages and careers makes me smile on the inside. But the best of friends you could ever receive are a dime a dozen.

Speaking of great friends Mike and Janette are just that in a nutshell. I truly pray for Mike because Janette is comedy gold to watch. I've never laughed so much in one sitting watching someone get their point across. That's the kind of friendship I cherish everyday that I wake.

The last and best friendship I'm thankful for is between me, my wife and God. That is the foundation of what keeps me sane day to day. That beauty that I married deserves nothing but the best. I'll spend the rest of my life doing just that. And I'll pray for Mike and Janette's antics. But I'm sure he'll live a long happy life full of laughter.

20

Conclusion

Yessss Mona was being honest with you, Janette is back with something else to say. If you want strong relationships like ours all you need is someone like me in your corner. The person who will tell you the truth and get you the instructions of how to overcome anything. Let me tell you guys something else about our marriages.

You want to know why the men in this family don't cheat? It's because they know I'm always looking out for the best interest of the women in this family. I'm sure you've seen the stories of my antics when women try to get with these fine men. I admit there is always a whoopin ready to be handed down to anyone who wants it from me. You know that my family laughs at my interrogation techniques but I am serious about every question I have to make people think.

You can always tell when a person has no home training out in public. They walk around like they are better than everyone else or those who are so conceited that you can smell their low self-esteem before you get in the room. Most of the women and men that act this way have never been taught to stay in their own lane or how to back down when in the presence of a crazy woman like myself. I'm not the one to play with, I will beat some respect and common sense into you real quick.

 I shouldn't have gone off on that rant on the page but, my favorite author K.Moore just lets me vent. I'm going to get out of here for now and let you talk to my bestie again. But don't think I'm leaving anytime soon because I'll be back to drop some knowledge on the young people. Bye now I'll see you guys in book 10: 4 seasons of Love.

My bestie was not kidding with you guys. We'll be

giving you guys some romance advice in book 10. We'll also be giving you guys some marriage advice in book 11: Marriage Anonymous. These two grandmas are just a book away if you ever get bored and need some entertainment.

Thank you for supporting our family and I hope you enjoyed reading this series. Like my bestie said, K.Moore is our favorite author. Please support her. Check out the next 6 books in this author's collection. She will inspire you. She proves that the underdog can always be a winner in the end.

I said it before and I'll say it again " see you later guys". Until we meet up again **Happy Reading** to you all in the reading world. A huge thank you from **(The Williams, Smith, Byrd, Lewis, Ramirez and Stuart)** Families.

21

Introduction to book 9

(Ezekiel) I want to have a one on one conversation with you trauma victims out there. Whether it be physical, emotional, psychological, mental. In this book my wife and I will share our trauma and the ways we overcame it. We're each going to write a personal letter to give you the strength to survive.

Message from the Author

I hope that this Bonded by Love series helps my readers out there build relationships with their families. I also hope you build stronger friendships with those around you.   Lastly I hope you all build your Christian relationship with our heavenly father above.

Contact Me

E-Mail: relatablefictionwriting@gmail.com

tik tok: LeavingTraumabehind4

X: LeavingTrauma4

Facebook: nakeialdavis-moore

instagram: soultavern_owner2020

About the Author

K.Moore is the mastermind of relatable fiction writing for your reading pleasure. The beginning of my writing journey started in 2024 with the Leaving Trauma Behind Series. I am a single mother of 1 with a background in Customer Service. This Bonded by Love Series is a continuation in my writing journey. There are more stories to come from me **Stay Tuned** as I complete this storyline with all of my characters.

Printed by Libri Plureos GmbH in Hamburg, Germany